Let's Be Kind

P. K. Hallinan

ideals children's books®

Nashville, Tennessee

ISBN-13: 978-0-8249-5605-9

Published by Ideals Children's Books
An imprint of Ideals Publications
A Guideposts Company
Nashville, Tennessee
www.idealsbooks.com

Color separations by Precision Color Graphics, Franklin, Wisconsin
Printed and bound in the United States of America

Library of Congress CIP data on file

Designed by Georgina Chidlow-Rucker

10 9 8 7 6 5 4 3 2 1

This book is for

_____

◆ ◆ ◆

From

_____

I like to be kind; it's a nice thing to be.
When I reach out to others . . .

They reach back to me!

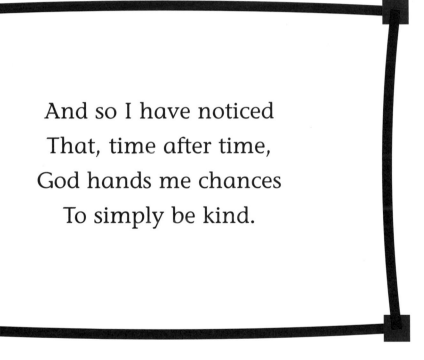

And so I have noticed
That, time after time,
God hands me chances
To simply be kind.

I'm kind to my family—I pick up my toys.

I go out-of-doors when I want to make noise!

But whenever they need me,
I'm always right there
To help them feel better
And to show them I care.

I'm kind to my friends—I do all I can
To be a good listener . . .

And to lend them a hand.

And when problems come,
I know it's a must
To shine with a kindness
They can lean on and trust.

I'm kind, too, to strangers,
When Mommy's nearby.
I offer a smile, and I always say, "Hi!"

And I'm kind to our neighbors
And bring them a treat
Whenever they're ailing—or just need to eat.

And always I'm kind
To God's animals too,
For their care is entrusted
To me and to you.

Yes, I'm kind to the lonely,
The hurting, the lost.

I'm kind without minding—
Whatever the cost.

For God blesses kindness in so many ways,
That the kindness I give out is always repaid!

So this much is certain: I know I will find
The happiest life . . .

By just being kind.